THE AZTEC EMPIRE

*W*ith special thanks to Dr. Charles S. Spencer,
Curator of Mexican and Central American Archaeology at the
American Museum of Natural History, New York,
for his expert assistance

CULTURES
OF THE PAST

THE
AZTEC
EMPIRE

R. CONRAD STEIN

BENCHMARK BOOKS

MARSHALL CAVENDISH
NEW YORK

Benchmark Books
Marshall Cavendish Corporation
99 White Plains Road
Tarrytown, New York 10591-9001

Library of Congress Cataloging-in-Publication Data
Stein, R. Conrad.
        The Aztec empire / by R. Conrad Stein.
                p.   cm.—(Cultures of the past)
        Includes bibliographical references and index.
        ISBN 0-7614-0072-9
        1. Aztecs—Juvenile literature. [1. Aztecs. 2. Indians of Mexico.] I. Title
II. Series.
        F1219.73.S76   1996
        972'.018—dc20   95-7333

SUMMARY: Traces the Aztec Empire from its beginnings in the deserts of northern
Mexico to its conquest by Hernán Cortés, discussing the history, culture, deities, and
legacy of the Aztecs.

Printed and bound in Italy

Book design by Carol Matsuyama
Photo research by Debbie Needleman

Front cover: Diego Rivera's mural of life in the Aztec capital, Tenochtitlán.
Back cover: A modern artist's depiction of Tenochtitlán at the time of the Spanish
    conquest.

Photo Credits
Front cover: courtesy of Nik Wheeler; back cover: courtesy of Robert Frerck/
Odyssey Productions/Hillstrom Stock Photo; pages 6, 12, 21, 27, 62, 64, 68: Robert
Frerck/Odyssey Productions/Hillstrom Stock Photo; pages 9, 28, 38, 39, 48, 53, 57,
63, 65, 66, 70: David Hiser, Photographers/Aspen; page 11: *Codex Mendoza,*
MS. Arch. Selden. A.1, The Bodleian Library, Oxford; pages 14 *(top),* 17, 35: Laurie
Platt Winfrey, Inc.; page 14 *(bottom):* Bridgeman/Art Resource, NY; page 19: The
Bettmann Archive; page 20: The St. Louis Art Museum, Gift of Morton D. May; page
22: Edward E. Ayer Collection, The Newberry Library; pages 25, 72: Nik Wheeler;
pages 26, 36: Robert Somerlott; page 30: Louis S. Glanzman/National Geographic
Society; page 41: Kevin Schafer/Hillstrom Stock Photo; page 44: SEF/Art Resource,
NY; page 46: Biblioteca Nazionale Centrale, Florence/Bridgeman Art Library,
London; page 52: Bibliothéque Nationale, Paris/Bridgeman Art Library, London;
pages 42, 47, 59: Werner Forman/Art Resource, NY; page 49: Scala/Art Resource,
NY; page 56: John Bigelow Taylor/Art Resource, NY; page 58: Victor Boswell/
National Geographic Society; page 60: Kenneth Garrett/National Geographic Society;
page 69: Michael Zabe/Art Resource, NY

CONTENTS

CHAPTER ONE

THE PROMISE OF A GOD

ong ago, according to an Aztec legend, the people lived in a wonderful land called Aztlán (AHZ-tlahn). Aztlán lay somewhere in northern Mexico. The legend claimed it was like the Garden of Eden. It had rushing rivers, lakes teeming with fish, and beautiful wildflowers covering the ground. Then, quite suddenly, the Aztecs were forced to leave Aztlán. The legend gives no clue as to why they abandoned this paradise on earth. In modern times, archaeologists (men and women who study ancient societies) have tried to find the site of old Aztlán. They have had no success in their search for this magical land.

The Wandering Period

With the gates of paradise closed behind them, the Aztecs wandered in the deserts of northern Mexico. It was a hostile region of cactus and rocks. Often the people were forced to eat snakes and lizards.

As was true in many ancient societies, the Aztecs believed in a great number of gods. While living in the desert they adopted a

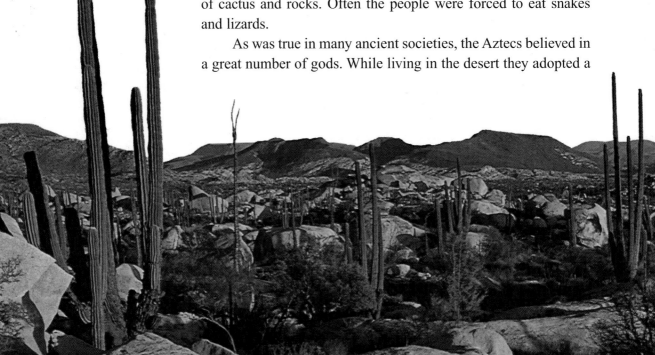

WHERE WAS AZTLÁN?

Searching for Aztlán is an ancient effort. More than five hundred years ago, the Aztec government sent an expedition to the north to find the nation's legendary homeland. The expedition found nothing to verify the old story. In modern times theories have been advanced suggesting that Aztlán was located as far north as the American state of Wisconsin. Surely the ancient paradise that sounds so much like the Biblical Garden of Eden had to be near a river or a lake. Aztec writers often claimed the people of Aztlán regularly feasted on fish and ducks. Today many scholars believe Aztlán was a settlement along the San Pedro River, about 450 miles northwest of Mexico City. But no one can be certain of the location. Nor do we know for sure if the marvelous Aztlán ever existed at all.

new god with the tongue-twisting name Huitzilopochtli (wheet-zee-loh-POHS-tlee). In the Aztec language, the name meant "Hummingbird on the Left." The Aztecs probably borrowed this deity from other peoples living in northern Mexico. A god similar to Huitzilopochtli was worshiped by several tribes in the area.

As they trekked over the desert, the Aztecs carried a wooden statue of the Hummingbird in a cagelike platform. The statue was the most precious object the wanderers possessed. During secret rituals, high priests said they were able to speak to the god

According to their historians, the Aztecs left Aztlán and wandered in a desert such as this for one hundred years before they saw the sign from a god commanding them to build a city.

through the statue. According to the priests, the Hummingbird issued precise instructions to the Aztec people: They should continue roving the desert until they saw an eagle eating a snake while sitting on a cactus. On that spot they must build a city. The god promised that the city would become the capital of a vast empire.

Tribal historians claim the Aztecs remained desert nomads for more than a century. But though still hungry and homeless, they now had hope. The promise of the Hummingbird gave their ordeal a glorious purpose. Some day they would find the eagle, the cactus, and the snake. Then they would have a home forever after. In the words of an ancient poem, the Hummingbird god said, "Let my children suffer and weep now/But their time will come."

The long wandering period strengthened the Aztec people in two ways: First, it gave them an intense desire to protect their homeland once they finally found a place to settle. The desert memory was a painful one for the Aztecs. Never again, they vowed, would they become a homeless band drifting over empty land. Second, the mere act of surviving the desert toughened the people. In the future their army would fight with a brand of desperate courage never before seen in Mexico.

Priests claimed the Hummingbird gave the tribe a general direction in which to travel. The god commanded them to keep the Gulf of Mexico on their left as they walked. For that reason he was called Hummingbird on the Left. Obeying the command the Aztecs moved steadily south. The direction took them out of northern Mexico and toward a promised land.

The Valley of Mexico

It was probably in the year 1248 that the Aztecs first entered the Valley of Mexico. The valley was a bowl-shaped depression, about forty miles wide, that lay like a nest in the mountains. Today Mexico City sprawls over the southern end of that valley. For centuries the fertile valley had nourished farming civilizations that reached great heights of culture. The Aztecs were astounded to see cities of stone houses clustered around pyramids built in honor of the gods. Never had the wandering tribe dreamed such cities as these existed.

The people living in the Valley of Mexico wrote reports about the newcomers from the north. Because of those written records, we know the Aztecs arrived sometime near the year 1248. We also know the city dwellers were not pleased with the sudden strangers in their midst. They described the Aztecs as brutes who were lacking in manners, a people not to be trusted. One ancient writer complained, "They [the Aztecs] had no houses, they had no land, they had no woven capes as clothing."

At the time, the Valley of Mexico rocked with warfare. One hundred years earlier, a powerful society called the Toltecs had ruled much of the valley. The Toltec culture declined, however,

The remains of a temple built by the Toltec people, who rose to power before the Aztecs settled in the Valley of Mexico. The Aztecs adopted many Toltec customs and began worshiping Toltec gods.

leaving the region with many small city-states that were almost constantly at war with one another. The perpetual wars provided the Aztecs a livelihood. Though the settled people regarded the Aztecs as barbarians, they respected their fierce fighting abilities. Decades of trekking in the desert had hardened the people, making them ideal soldiers. The city-states hired Aztec men to fight their battles. These men became mercenaries, soldiers who fought for pay.

When not fighting other people's wars, the Aztecs continued to roam central Mexico, living off the land. During peacetime they were unwelcome as neighbors by most city-states. The outcasts found friends only when war loomed.

Then, in the year 1325, the Aztecs came upon an island in the broad but shallow Lake Texcoco (tay-SKOH-koh), which spread over the southern end of the valley. On the island they claimed to see a miracle: An eagle sat on a cactus while devouring a snake. Here was the long-awaited sign from the heavens that commanded them to build a city. Now they had found a home and were free to seek the glory promised them by their Hummingbird god.

Empire Building

For two centuries after the miracle of the cactus, the Aztecs concentrated on two activities—they built a grandiose capital city, and they relentlessly expanded their territory. They named their city Tenochtitlán (tay-nahk-tee-TLAHN), meaning "Place of the Cactus." As they constructed the capital, their ruthlessly efficient army conquered neighboring city-states.

In Tenochtitlán workers drained marshes and cut canals through the island settlement. Being a military society, the Aztecs worked in a disciplined and orderly fashion. Canals were laid out in a gridlike manner similar to the streets in an American city. Broad causeways were constructed to allow foot traffic from the island to the mainland. Engineers expanded the island by sinking timbers out in the waters and filling in the gaps with boulders and mud. Soldier immigrants from neighboring tribes poured in, seeking Aztec citizenship. By the 1450s, a little more than one hundred years after its founding, Tenochtitlán held about seventy

An Aztec account of the founding of Tenochtitlán in the year 1325. At the center of this drawing is an eagle perched on a cactus.

thousand inhabitants. Beholding its grace and beauty, an Aztec poet wrote:

> The city is spread out in circles of jade,
> radiating flashes of light like quetzal
> (keht-SUHL) feathers,
> Beside it the lords are borne in boats:
> over them extends a flowery mist.

From their base at Tenochtitlán the Aztecs pushed outward, gaining territory in every direction. First they became the dominant power in the Valley of Mexico. One by one the city-states, which had employed the Aztec army as mercenaries, now fell before that same army. When they chose not to fight, the Aztecs entered into alliances with powerful city-states. Then, as their strength grew, the Aztecs ignored the terms of the alliances and made their allies their vassals. After securing the Valley of Mexico, Aztec territory continued to spread. By the early 1500s the empire

The island city of Tenochtitlán, with its gridlike network of canals

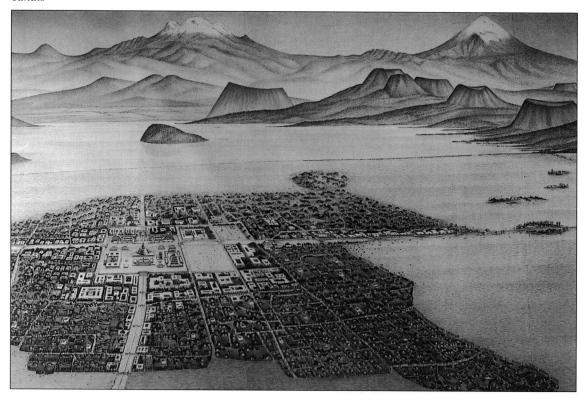

ranged from the Gulf of Mexico to the Pacific Ocean, south to the jungles of Central America, and north to the desert land. Historians estimate that anywhere from five to six million people lived under Aztec rule.

Spearheading Aztec expansion was a splendid army. The nation's leaders studied war and elevated the practice to a science. Some historians believe the Aztecs were the first soldiers in the Americas to fight with swords. Bravery was instilled in their men. At birth a tiny bow and arrow was placed in a boy's hand and a poem read over his crib:

> *Loved and tender son,*
> *This is the will of the gods.*
> *You are not born in your true house,*
> *Because you are a warrior . . .*
> *You are promised to the field of battle.*
> *You are dedicated to war.*

In the early 1500s an emperor named Montezuma (also spelled Moctezuma or Motecuhzoma) presided over the Aztec nation. Montezuma was a high priest, trained in the mysteries and magic of the Aztec religion. Like all Aztecs, he worshiped many gods. He also believed that strange or unexpected events foretold either good fortune or doom for his nation. In the early 1500s the empire was beset by a series of confusing signs. A comet that baffled Aztec astronomers hung in the sky night after night. The wooden temple that stood on top of the tall pyramid of the Hummingbird mysteriously caught fire and burned to ashes despite the frantic efforts of workers to put out the blaze. On dark nights residents of the capital claimed they were awakened by the anguished voice of a woman crying out, "My children! My children! We are lost."

Montezuma felt he was king of all the world. Yet the puzzling events taking place in his kingdom haunted him. He summoned astrologers, magicians, and priests to his court and asked them to determine the meaning of the signs. They gave him confusing answers, leaving Montezuma to wonder if he somehow had offended a powerful god.

The crowning of Emperor Montezuma. This ceremony would have taken place in the year 1502.

It is thought that this headdress was once worn by Montezuma. The Aztecs valued brightly colored rare feathers higher than they did gold.

The God from the East

From Europe, in the Old World far to the east, Spanish soldiers riding great ships began probing the eastern shores of Mexico. Spaniards had already colonized the Caribbean islands of Hispaniola (today's Haiti and Dominican Republic), Puerto Rico, and Cuba. Like the Aztecs the Spaniards were a military society whose soldiers lusted for battle and whose leaders hungered for more territory. In the New World the Spaniards sought conquest, gold, and souls to convert to Christianity. The Spanish soldiers were the conquistadores (conquerors). Historians have summed up their mission in the Americas in three words: God, gold, and glory.

One of the boldest of the conquistadores was an army commander named Hernán Cortés. In early 1519 Cortés landed on Mexican shores near the present-day city of Veracruz. Through a woman interpreter named Malinche (mah-LEEN-chay) and a Spanish sailor who had been shipwrecked in Mexico seven years earlier, Cortés was able to speak with the coastal people. He asked where he could find gold. The coastal people pointed inland and said, "Mexico! Mexico!" The Aztec people were also called the Mexica, and their capital city of Tenochtitlán was known on the coast as Mexico.

In August of 1519 Cortés began an incredible march 250 miles inland to the golden city called Mexico. His trek led through unknown regions in one of which he would face an enemy army numbering many thousands. Despite the risks, Cortés was determined to go forward with his plans. To make certain his troops would not mutiny and sail away from this fearsome situation, Cortés burned his fleet. By destroying the ships, he left his men with little choice but to follow their commander, even to death.

Through an ingenious system of runners Montezuma was informed of events taking place on his empire's eastern coast. He was told the leader of the invaders was a bearded man with white skin. The strangers rode on the backs of large deer (no one in Mexico had ever seen a horse before). They fought using sticks that cracked like thunder. Their chief preached a new religion.

Now Montezuma's darkest fears were confirmed. As a high priest, he knew well the story of Quetzalcóatl (kehts-uhl-KUH-wah-tl), a god who reportedly lived with the Mexican people in ancient times. In the old drawings Quetzalcóatl was often pictured

AZTEC TRACK STARS

It took Cortés and his army two-and-one-half months to march from the sea to Tenochtitlán. Teams of Aztec runners made the same trip in just twenty-four hours. The Aztecs communicated with their far-flung empire through a remarkable corps of runners who carried written messages. Individual runners raced over trails to post houses spaced about 5.2 miles apart. At the post house, one runner handed the message to a fresh runner, who rushed it to the next post house. The process was repeated until the message was delivered, and the long-range relay race came to an exhausting end. In this manner messages were carried at the incredible speed of 10 miles per hour. Sometimes the runners transported fish. If the emperor in Tenochtitlán had a whim for fresh fish from the ocean, he simply ordered one from his corps of runners. The runners, who were trained for their duties from birth, had a fish on the emperor's plate before it emitted a telltale scent of age.

as a bearded man with a white face. Legend had it that he intended to return in the year One Reed on the Aztec calendar and claim all of Mexico in his name. The year 1519, when Cortés arrived, coincided exactly with the Aztec year One Reed.

Desperately Montezuma tried to keep this powerful stranger from reaching Tenochtitlán. Through emissaries he sent gifts of gold: The gifts were intended to bribe Cortés into staying away from the Aztec capital. Cortés simply kept the gold and continued his march. Montezuma arranged for an ambush at the city of Cholula, some sixty miles from Tenochtitlán. Cortés, however, got wind of the ambush and slaughtered the enemy soldiers. In Montezuma's mind the white foreigner was unstoppable in his determination to enter the gates of Tenochtitlán. Surely he must be a god.

In November 1519 Cortés arrived at the Aztec capital. There he was greeted by Montezuma. It marked the first time in history that a European had met the head of a grand nation in the Americas. The meeting was cordial, even friendly. Cortés took a pearl necklace off his own neck and gave it to Montezuma. The Aztec leader presented Cortés with eight golden pieces delicately cast in the shape of shrimps.

A Short-Lived Peace

Peaceful relations between Aztecs and Spaniards lasted only nine days, however. In a fit of temper the brash Cortés seized Montezuma and held him captive in the emperor's own palace. Aztec generals, many of whom still believed Cortés was a god, were too shocked by this outrageous act to fight back. For a strange six-month period Cortés kept Montezuma a prisoner and ruled the Aztec empire himself. Finally the Aztecs rebelled. After bitter fighting they drove the Spaniards from their capital city. Montezuma was killed during the uprising. Leadership of the Aztec empire fell to his nephew Cuauhtémoc (kwau-TEHM-ohk). Also hundreds of Spaniards, who were overburdened with gold they stole from the Aztec treasury, drowned in Lake Texcoco while fleeing the capital.

Cortés fumed at the defeat. For a full year he concentrated on

Hernán Cortés. The Aztecs believed he was their pale-faced, bearded god Quetzalcóatl, returning to claim the land.

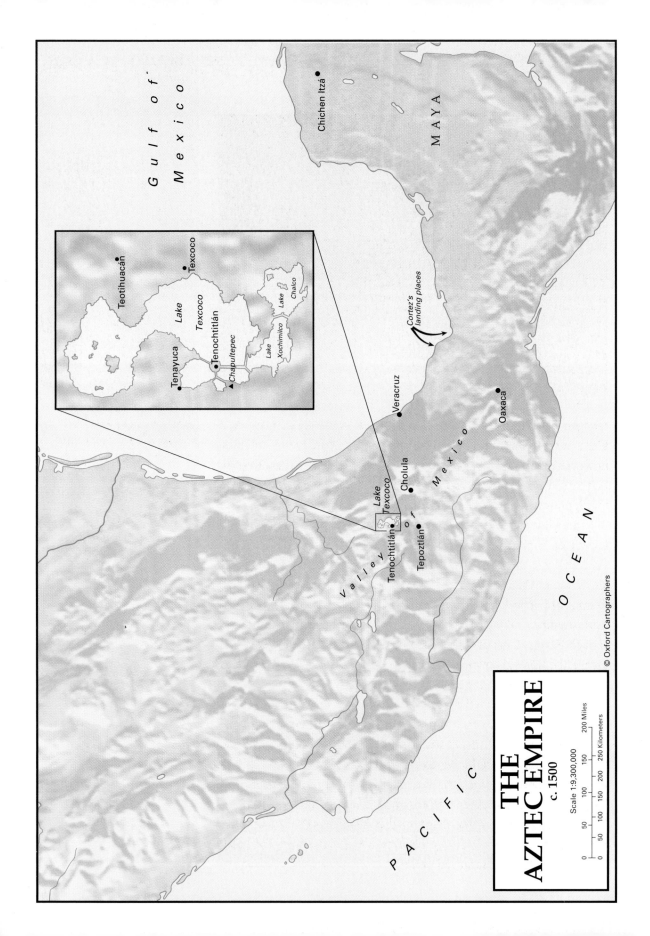

Gulf of Mexico

Chichen Itzá

MAYA

Teotihuacán

Texcoco

Lake Texcoco

Lake Chalco

Tenayuca

Tenochtitlán

Chapultepec

Lake Xochimilco

Cortez's landing places

Veracruz

Oaxaca

Cholula

Valley

Lake Texcoco

of

Mexico

Tenochtitlán

Tepoztlán

OCEAN

PACIFIC

© Oxford Cartographers

THE
AZTEC EMPIRE
c. 1500

Scale 1:9,300,000

| 0 | 50 | 100 | 150 | 200 Miles |

| 0 | 50 | 100 | 150 | 200 | 250 Kilometers |

The meeting between Montezuma and Cortés in 1519, painted by a Spanish artist many years later

reorganizing his army. More Spaniards arrived on the coast and were recruited into his ranks. The vast majority of Cortés's soldiers, however, came from within the Aztec empire. The vassal nations had long tired of paying taxes to Aztec overlords and eagerly joined the Spaniards in their effort to crush the hated rulers.

In May of 1521 the Spaniards and their Indian allies attacked the Aztec capital of Tenochtitlán. A terrible battle broke out that lasted almost three months. The Aztec people within the city were surrounded. Besides having stronger weapons than the Aztecs, the Spaniards carried, unwittingly, another powerful force for destruction: smallpox. The Aztec people died of disease and starvation by the thousands. Corpses blackened the streets and the canals. A soldier in the Spanish army wrote, "We could not walk without treading on the bodies and the heads of dead Indians."

Fighting within the city raged from house to house and spread to the towering pyramids. True to their military traditions, the Aztecs fought till death for every stone of Tenochtitlán. When the battle finally concluded, the great city was reduced to smoking ruins. The surviving Aztecs, numbed by the defeat, moved like ghosts over the ashes of their once-great capital. The death of Tenochtitlán heralded the death of the Aztec world. The empire, promised to the people for an eternity by the Hummingbird god, had lasted only two hundred years.

CHAPTER TWO

THE AZTEC WORLD

Throughout their history the Aztecs were a military society. As was true in most military societies, life in the Aztec world was often cruel. Judges sentenced people to death for such trifling offenses as drunkenness. Aztec children, especially boys, were subjected to painful punishments. Fathers held a disobedient boy's face over a smoky fire that was laced with chili peppers, thereby forcing the child to breathe spicy hot smoke.

Yet the Aztec world enjoyed a richness that rose above its harsh military order. The Aztecs were builders who assembled one of the greatest cities ever known. They were poets who sought immortality in the written line. And they were a people who loved to celebrate life. They regularly held grand festivals that enlisted the entire population of a city as active guests. The Aztec world was alive with art, music, and excitement.

Tenochtitlán, the Dream City

In 1519 the Spanish soldiers under Cortés entered the Aztec capital, shaking their heads in amazement. They marveled at pyramids that rose taller than any church spire in Spain. They saw palaces supporting rooftop gardens that overflowed with flowers. They walked on streets that were ruler straight and kept spotlessly clean. The city itself was large beyond their imaginations. At the time the Spaniards arrived, it held more than 200,000 people and contained some sixty thousand buildings. No city in all of Europe was bigger.

A Spanish soldier named Bernal Díaz del Castillo later wrote

An Aztec sculptor crafted this man, who was probably a merchant, carrying a load of corn.

A painting showing Tenochtitlán as it looked at the time of the Conquest. The tallest pyramid in the center is devoted to the Hummingbird god.

a book about what he saw in the land of the Aztecs. When Díaz described his first glimpse of Tenochtitlán, he sounded like a man awestruck, as if he were visiting a faraway planet:

> *When we beheld the broad causeway running straight and level to the city, we could compare it to nothing but the enchanted scenes we had read of. . . . Great towers and temples, and other edifices of lime and stone seemed to rise out of the water. To many of us it appeared doubtful whether we were asleep or awake . . . for it must be considered that never before did man see, hear, or dream of anything equal to the spectacle which appeared to our eyes on this day.*

We too can only dream about the marvelous city of the past. The great capital was totally destroyed in the battle between Aztecs and Spaniards. Immediately after the battle, the Spaniards began to build Mexico City on top of the rubble of Tenochtitlán. Some of the older buildings that stand in today's Mexico City were built from bricks that once made up the walls of pyramids or palaces. Yet the overall design of the old city was not lost. Through manuscripts and drawings, both Spanish and Aztec, it is possible to recreate the dream city that was once the hub of an empire.

Tenochtitlán was about five square miles in size. It was an island city, surrounded on all sides by the waters of Lake Texcoco. Today most of that lake has dried up. Modern Mexico City, ironically, suffers from a shortage of water. Five hundred years ago, the lake was diamond clear and teemed with fish and waterfowl. The Aztecs kept the lake clean through a system of carrying away human waste and using it as fertilizer. Thus the Aztecs practiced sewage treatment long before the concept was considered in Europe.

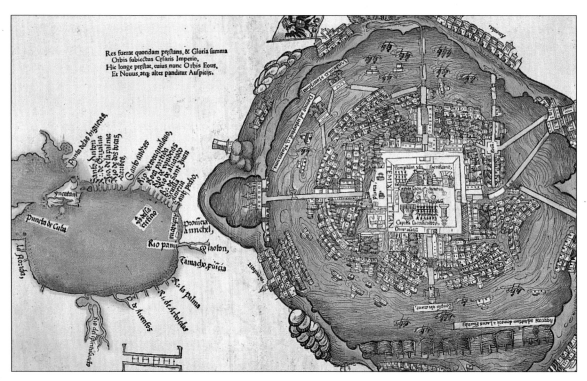

This map of old Tenochtitlán may have been drawn by Cortés.

Canals were essential to Tenochtitlán's commerce. The Aztecs had no domestic animals, such as oxen or horses, that could be used to pull carts. For that reason they had little need for the wheel. In Aztec society, wheels were used mostly on colorful toy wagons that children pushed over the ground. Through the canals, merchants in boats brought goods to the city's marketplace. Some of the boats were large enough to carry sixty people

Bernal Díaz del Castillo was a young foot soldier who served in the army of Hernán Cortés. When he was in his seventies, he wrote a book, *The True History of the Conquest of Mexico*, that told of his adventures. Díaz was privileged to see the Aztec empire in all its glory before it was vanquished by the Spaniards. He was one of the few eyewitnesses to write an accurate account of the empire. Cortés's own reports were self-serving. The commander tended to glorify his role in the conquest in order to impress the Spanish king. Aztec writers were poets rather than reporters, and they rarely described everyday sights such as the market and the temple complex at Tenochtitlán. Bernal Díaz did concentrate on such details. His book is the most readable firsthand account we have of the great empire that existed long ago.

or an equivalent weight in goods. Concrete causeways, built by Aztec engineers, allowed foot traffic between the island city and the mainland. Cortés claimed that the causeways were wide enough to permit eight horsemen to ride abreast. Each causeway contained a series of drawbridges that were raised or removed so that boats could pass.

In the center of the great city rose the pyramid complex where all the major pyramids and temples stood. The area was surrounded by an eight-foot stone wall that was topped by carvings of snakes. The tallest of the pyramids was that belonging to Huitzilopochtli, the Hummingbird god. His shrine rose to the height of a modern eight-story building, and its base covered two acres of ground. Nearby stood the temple of another powerful deity: Tlaloc, the god of rain. In central Mexico, where rain was precious, Tlaloc was a mighty force.

The palaces and rambling houses of noble families were located near the temple enclosure. Biggest of the houses was that belonging to the emperor, which Spanish reports say contained one hundred rooms and three large plazas. Walls inside the grand houses were bedecked with rare woods, specially selected to be sweet smelling. Statues of mythical animals such as winged mountain lions stood in the hallways. Rooms were built in a circle around an open patio, which usually had a fountain in the middle. Bernal Díaz, the humble Spanish soldier, never ceased to praise "the appearance of the palaces . . . how spacious and well-built . . . of beautiful stonework . . . with great rooms and courts, all a wonder to behold."

Common people lived in stone houses with thatched roofs. Often the outsides of the houses were whitewashed, giving the city a silvery hue that dazzled the Spaniards. The insides, however, were cramped, dark, and smoky from kitchen fires. A worker's house was made up of one large room with a dirt floor. Most were windowless because people were afraid the night air contained evil spirits that could slip through any opening. The Aztec worker who could not afford stone lived in a house made of reeds and covered with a plaster of mud.

The Marketplace, the Pulsing Hub of Life

Buzzing with activity and alive with color, the marketplace of Tenochtitlán was the city's heart. The market was a broad, open plaza, where as many as sixty thousand people gathered to shop or just to socialize. All the goods available in the empire were bought and sold there. Most vendors sat on the ground, displaying their merchandise spread out on woven mats. Often they shouted out prices. Bernal Díaz claimed one vendor had such a booming voice, "he could be heard for more than a league." A league is roughly three miles.

Some vendors sold ornaments and jewelry made of gold. The Spaniards, always hungry for gold, took particular interest in the jewelry offered for sale. They claimed the Aztec goldsmiths were as skilled as those in Europe. Said one conquistador, "They can cast [in gold] a parrot that moves its tongue, head, and wings; a monkey that moves its feet and head. . . ."

MONTEZUMA'S ZOO

Emperor Montezuma enjoyed a private zoo on his palace grounds. The zoo's aviary section contained examples of all the birds known in the Aztec empire. Many hundreds of workers cleaned the aviary's cages and fed the birds. Special veterinarians tended to birds that became ill. Other cages held jaguars, ocelots, and monkeys from the south. Wolves, bears, and mountain lions from the northern limits of Aztec territory also paced about in cages inside the emperor's zoo.

The great Mexican muralist Diego Rivera (1886–1957) painted this scene of what life might have been like in the Aztec capital.

The Aztecs valued brightly colored feathers even more than they did gold. Among the most prized articles at the market were wall hangings made by sewing feathers onto cloth. The finest of these pieces used the emerald green feathers of the quetzal, a rare bird found in the jungles to the south. A Spaniard reported, "They will make a butterfly, an animal, a tree, a rose, flowers, herbs, and rocks, all done with feathers, and with such fidelity they seem alive and natural."

Displaying a love for order and harmony, the Aztecs divided the market into sections. One section was devoted to vegetables— sweet potatoes, avocados, and squash. A neighboring section held fish. Another section offered brightly colored cotton cloth. In still another section, men and women sold honey in pottery jars.

Gold jewelry created by Aztec craftsmen. Spanish soldiers claimed that Aztec jewelers were as skilled as those in Europe.

26

Barbers cut hair in stalls. Cooks served food in tiny restaurants. Doctors examined patients in open-air offices. Herb sellers sold concoctions that they guaranteed would cure such ills as sleeplessness or coughing. Men and women slaves were sold at the market. Bernal Díaz said the slaves "were tied to long poles, with collars around their necks so they would not escape."

The Aztecs had no coins or paper money. Instead they used cacao beans as a means of exchange. Often goods were bartered and no beans changed hands. Arguments between buyers and sellers broke out, but usually the bantering was friendly. Anyone believing he or she was cheated could sue in a special court that served the market only. The judge at the market court listened to both arguments and handed down immediate decisions. Stealing of goods was not tolerated. A petty thief was punished by having his head shaved. Stealing valuable items such as gold or feathers carried stiffer penalties: condemnation to slavery or death. A death sentence was carried out on the spot, often with the offender having his head crushed between two large rocks.

In this model of an Aztec market, Tenochtitlán comes to life.

Food and Farming

The Valley of Mexico is blessed with one of the most pleasant climates found anywhere on earth. Sunshine is almost constant and frost and snow are rare. For farmers, this means a long growing season with few freaks of weather that can destroy crops. But this ideal setting for farmers is flawed by lack of rainfall. Rain over central Mexico is seasonal. The rainy season begins in June and lasts until September. If rain does not fall during that four-month period, a disaster awaits the farmer and those who depend on the farmer for food. The Aztecs looked upon their rain god as a powerful but evil figure.

To counter the unsteady rainfall, the Aztecs built unique "floating gardens" in the lakes of the Valley of Mexico. The gardens, called *chinampas* (chee-NAHM-pas), were made by placing retaining walls in the lake waters and filling them in with mud, reeds, and rotting vegetables. Thus an island was created on the lake. The island was topped with a layer of dirt, and farmers

Xochimilco, a "floating garden" still in use in Mexico today

planted vegetables on the surface. Seepage from the retaining walls irrigated the crops. Tree saplings were placed on the corners of these vegetable beds, and soon trees took root on the lake bottom. Because of the tree roots embedded in the lake, the gardens did not really "float." Fully three-quarters of the surface of some lakes in the Valley of Mexico were covered with *chinampas*. It was an ingenious way to farm. Instead of bringing water to the land, the *chinampa* system allowed a farmer to bring land to the water. The special farms-on-the-lake were highly productive. *Chinampas* regularly produced two crops of vegetables a year.

Corn was the staple food for the Aztecs. Dried corn lasted a year or more in storage, making it ideal as a source of food for all seasons. The dried corn was ground up in stone basins and patted into corn cakes. Today these corn cakes, *tortillas,* remain the common bread of Mexico. Along with corn cakes, the Aztecs ate various forms of beans. Their favorite flavoring spice was the chili pepper. At the market, chilis were separated by size, color, and heat. Biting into the hottest of the peppers was like tasting fire and made tears run out of one's eyes. People ate fish or wild fowl on occasion. Nobles ate deer meat and the meat from domestic dogs and turkeys. Rarely did the common people taste meat at all.

Education—Discipline in a Military World

No boy in Aztec society was allowed to forget his role as a future soldier. At the age of six, a boy from the working classes was separated from his family and sent to a boarding school called a *telpochcalli* (tehl-pohsh-KAH-lee). In school he learned history and religion but was not taught how to read. Reading and writing were skills reserved for the higher classes. The primary function of the *telpochcalli* was to prepare a boy for war. Students practiced spear-throwing, archery, and combat with clubs. Discipline was severe. A student was expected to punish himself for minor infractions by sticking a cactus spike through his earlobe or through his tongue. The American historian William Prescott, who wrote a well-known book about the period, remarked, "Terror, not love, was the spring of education for the Aztecs."

The sons of the wealthy attended a military school called the

An Aztec street scene. The children sitting in the doorway learning to read are probably students at the calmecac, *the school for upper-class boys.*

calmecac (KAHL-meh-kahk), a place with rules so strict the word translates as "House of Tears." There they learned how to read and write in the Aztec pictographic manner. Since these boys were destined to lead the nation, they were given classes in government, engineering, mathematics, philosophy, and the Aztec passion—poetry. The boys who went to the elite *calmecac* were looked upon as the empire's future army officers and therefore had to be braver and tougher than the common soldiers. To mold them into hardened fighting men, they were forced to sleep on bare brick floors and bathe in icy streams. Rarely did the boys enjoy a full night's sleep because their instructors regularly shook them awake and sent them on midnight hikes into the mountains.

Yet not all the lessons at the military schools pointed a boy in the direction of war. The students were also taught how to play music, sing, and dance. Young nobles in the *calmecac* learned the proper way to hold and smell flowers. These lessons must have been a welcome break from the normal rigors of school life.

For sports, the boys were encouraged to play a game that consisted of putting a hard rubber ball through a hoop without using the hands. The ball game was called *Tlachtli* (TLAHSH-tlee). It was a fast-moving team sport that the Aztecs probably learned from the Maya people to the south. The ball courts were always located toward the rear of a major temple, so it is believed the game had some sort of religious significance.

Rich or poor, all boys went to war at about the age of sixteen. At first the junior soldiers were relegated to carrying weapons and supplies during long marches. Soon they were immersed in battle. A long-standing custom demanded that a boy have his head shaved at the age of ten, leaving only one lock of hair that hung down to his neck. He was not permitted to cut that lock until he had experienced war and had taken at least one prisoner.

The Role of Women

Young girls, especially those from the poorer classes, almost never attended schools. Instead, girls were schooled in the domestic trades at home by their mothers. They learned how to grind corn and pat corn cakes with their hands. Weaving either cotton or cactus fiber was honored as a woman's occupation. At their mothers' sides girls practiced working a loom to create clothing for the family. Most girls were married by the age of sixteen, and the marriages were arranged by the families. An old Aztec saying, which read like a commandment, told young women, "When your parents give you a husband, do not be disrespectful to him—obey him!"

The Aztec preoccupation with war led women to suffer a second-class status. War, it was thought, was strictly a man's business, and waging war was the most important function of the nation. Yet women managed to assert their influence despite the restrictions placed on them. At the marketplace, women were shrewd vendors and often set the prices in family-run enterprises. Upper-class women were allowed to assist in some religious rituals, but they could not become as important as the priests. Ancient laws prohibited women from even speaking during religious ceremonies.

A Passion for Beauty

In every society poets tend to be rebels. Normally Aztec leaders demanded unthinking obedience from their subjects. Poets, however, were given special freedom to explore their feelings and to question the world around them. Surely the Aztec writer who created the poem below thought not of his duties toward society. Instead he pondered the meaning of life and lamented its brevity:

> *We have come only to sleep.*
> *We have come only to dream.*
> *It is not true, it is not true*
> *That we have come to live on earth.*

> *As at every spring the grass is renewed,*
> *So do we too acquire form.*
> *Our heart puts out shoots, grows green.*
> *Our body begats a few flowers*
> *And then lies withered.*

IF YOU LIVED IN THE AZTEC CAPITAL

If you had been born in the Aztec capital city of Tenochtitlán, your way of life would have been determined by the facts of your birth—whether you were a girl or a boy; free or slave; wealthy or poor. With this chart you can trace the course your life might have taken as a member of upper-class Aztec society.

You were born in Tenochtitlán. . . .

As a Boy . . .

As a Girl . . .

You live in a palace where many rooms surround an open courtyard graced by a bubbling fountain. Your toys include straw or carved wooden figures of rabbits and birds as well as a wheeled wagon that you push along the ground. You are well cared for by your family and servants.

At age 6 you are separated from your family and sent to a *calmecac,* a military school where you are trained to be an officer in the Aztec army. Discipline is strict. As a self-punishment, you are expected to stick thorns through your tongue or your earlobes. Being upper class, you learn how to read and write; lower-class boys are denied that privilege.

At age 6 you begin to learn household tasks at home from your mother and servants. Because you are a female, you will not attend a formal school and will most likely never learn to read or write. At about age 8 you learn to spin cotton into cloth. Weaving is considered an honorable task for girls and women, even those of the upper classes.

At age 16 you go to war with the Aztec army. At first, as a novice soldier, you carry weapons or supplies during the long marches. You experience battle at about age 18. Bravery is expected. Any sign of cowardice in the heat of war is an unthinkable disgrace.

In your early teens, as an unmarried girl, you are chaperoned wherever you go. You are required to walk with your head bent, eyes on the ground, and speak only when spoken to. At about age 16 you will get married. Your husband will be picked by your parents with help from a matchmaker.

In your late teens or early 20s you get married. Your wife is chosen for you by your parents. As a member of the ruling class, you have some choice over your career: you can either enter government service or become a professional army officer. If you are an especially fine student, you can be chosen by priests to join them in the priesthood. You lead an active public life.

As a wife and mother you have little choice but to obey your husband's every command. You lead a life centered around the home and family. If your husband dies you are expected to remarry. Tradition demands that you marry one of your husband's relatives—a brother or a cousin. When you are older, you may become a community matchmaker yourself.

Both men and women are considered to be old at age 50. Few people in Aztec society reach that age. As an elder you are especially revered by your family. People value your advice because it is thought that years provide wisdom.

When you die you may be buried or cremated. Your body, dressed in the finest clothes, is displayed for four days while friends and relatives feast and chant prayers. Death is not a particularly sad event; rather, it is regarded as a stepping-stone into a new and usually better life.

One of the most revered poets in the empire's history was Nezahualcoyotl (neht-zah-whahl-KOY-oh-tl), the king of a city that neighbored Tenochtitlán. He was a true rebel. Through his poetry he even dared to suggest the concept of one god more powerful than all the gods the people worshiped. This omnipotent god was a mystery to humans. He did not answer prayers directly, and his favor could not be won by sacrifice. As king, Nezahual-coyotl ordered that no statue ever be made of this supreme deity. He did, however, praise the invisible god in his poetry:

> *God, our Lord, is invoked everywhere.*
> *Everywhere is He venerated.*
> *It is He who creates things,*
> *He creates Himself: God.*

In the Aztec world poems were spoken aloud to gatherings of listeners. Great poems were memorized and passed on from generation to generation. The nation's poets were hailed as intellectuals.

Despite their love of poetry the Aztecs found that it was difficult to convey the feeling behind a poem in their picture language. For that reason, poems were recited more often than written. However, the Aztec written language was efficient for record keeping and for the recording of historical events. Warfare often cropped up in the nation's historical records. The written symbol for war was a picture of a shield and a club. If the writer wanted to refer to a war fought far away, he simply drew the shield and club on the far side of the paper.

Religion dominated Aztec sculpture and painting. Their greatest statues were representations of the gods. Many of the gods had cold stares and ferocious expressions. Bernal Díaz said of the Hummingbird god's statue, "[It] had monstrous and terrible eyes . . . and the body was girded with snakes." Not all of the deities were so sinister looking, however. The goddess Tlazol-teotli (tlah-zohl-clih-OH-tlee) was the Aztec spirit associated with childbirth. A dramatic statue shows her squatting on the ground struggling to have a baby. Her face wears an expression of pain mixed with one of hope. The personalities of the gods burst forth from the statues, and their impact on human beings is great.

Xolotla (shoh-LOH-tlah), the god of death, appears in the form of a skeleton. A more cheerful goddess was Itzpapalotl (ihtz-pah-peh-LOH-tl), who is associated with butterflies; her statue has a flower poking out of a hole in her breast. Perhaps the flower served to nurture butterflies. In addition to gods and goddesses, Aztec sculptors fashioned ordinary creatures such as rabbits and eagles, and even flies and grasshoppers.

All of Aztec art displays a love for color. The Aztecs painted their statues, even those of the grim-faced gods. The inside walls of many Aztec homes were covered with paintings. Only a few of those wall paintings have survived, but the ones that can be seen today are a blaze of greens, yellows, and deep blues. Aztec legends depict a level of heaven as a vivid rainbow, bursting with reds and greens. Even the pictures in their written manuscripts are alive with color.

Tlazolteotli, the Aztec goddess of childbirth. Aztec sculpture was often very expressive.

The Excitement of the Festival

Warriors and their wives lead the parade. All wear strings of flowers crisscrossed around their chests. The warriors have on cloaks of brightly colored feathers. Particularly brave soldiers wear masks that resemble the faces of eagles or jaguars. They march down streets that children have strewn with flowers. Music plays—drums, rattles, and flutes. The long line of soldiers and their wives begins a dance. Their formation looks like a fantastic snake with colors radiating from its sides. It is the midsummer festival called Tlaxochimaco (tlahsh-oh-chih-MAH-koh), the

"Offering of the Flowers." Everyone in town watches the parade. Festival days are the most exciting, colorful times of the year.

Aztec festivals embraced all the people of a city neighborhood or a farming community. Almost always the festivals were religious in nature. They could be solemn. Many included human sacrifice, the ritualistic killing of human beings to please the gods. Others were devoted to pure joy, a celebration of life itself. Food was stored up so that all could feast during the great parties. Music, dance, and an explosion of color overwhelmed the Aztecs on festive days. The days set aside for celebration were carefully marked on the calendar, and everyone looked forward to them. Festivals heralded the coming of spring, the harvest, the feast day of a god, or perhaps the marriage of a royal daughter.

Games and staged events highlighted many of the great parties thrown by the Aztecs. During one festival men who wore the feathers of birds were swung on ropes down a long pole. The ceremony is still performed in Mexico today, and is called Los Voladores (lohs voh-lah-DOHR-ehs), "The Flyers." A game loved by young boys would begin when workers placed a large pole in the town square. Next, the town's boys gathered in a circle. At a signal they raced to the pole and began hurrying up ropes that were tied near the top. At the very top stood a paper image of a god. Each boy tried to reach the top first and bring down the image. The winner was given a special banquet. It was said the cleverest boy won by waiting. If the boy dallied on the ground for just a few minutes, he could scramble on the heads and shoulders of the others to get to the image first.

Looming above all festivals were statues of the gods, those unsmiling, often ferocious-looking figures who dominated Aztec society. The Aztecs did not separate religion from other aspects of their lives—farming, working, or waging war. To the Aztecs religion was life itself.

CHAPTER THREE

THE HUMANS AND THE GODS

We go, we walk along a very narrow road on earth.
On this side is an abyss, on that side is an abyss.
One goes, one walks, only in the middle.

These lines from an Aztec poem reflect the uncertainties of life. The lines also serve as a command: One should walk "only in the middle," where everyone else walks. Religion was the cornerstone of this lifestyle that called for all to march to the beat of the same drummer. The Aztecs could never escape their religion. Its stories, celebrations, and symbols were everywhere in their world.

Xiutecutl, the god of fire, sits brooding.

Myths with Meanings

Long ago, when the gods still lived on earth, a woman was sweeping the ground in front of a temple. She was the mother of four hundred sons. A pious woman, she revered the gods. While sweeping she discovered a ball of feathers on the steps and picked it up. She did not know the feathers had the magical power to make her pregnant. Her sons were furious when they discovered she would soon give birth. They were a jealous lot and refused to accept an addition to the family. The enraged children decided to kill their mother. But one of the four hundred sons managed to tell the unborn child, while he was still in the womb, of the murder plot against the mother. Suddenly the mother gave birth. Her child jumped forth, a full-grown man. Armed with a lightning bolt, he killed and drove away his angry brothers. He was Huitzilopochtli, the Hummingbird god. Born in war, he became the Aztec's guiding spirit for conquest.

The story of Huitzilopochtli is one of many myths told by the Aztec priests. The myths were powerful instruments for

Throughout Mexico, myths abounded that the people entered the world from caves—the wombs of the earth. Some scholars believe the ancient Mexicans built pyramids over particularly sacred caves.

WILLIAM H. PRESCOTT

The story of the Aztecs' rise and fall is so fascinating that it has been told and retold for hundreds of years. One of the finest chroniclers of the Aztec saga was the American writer William H. Prescott. Born in Massachusetts in 1796, Prescott suffered an accident as a young man that left him almost totally blind. To do the painstaking research for his history books, he paid clerks to read to him while he made mental notes. In 1843 he completed his masterpiece, *A History of the Conquest of Mexico.* He treated the conquest as if it were a sweeping adventure story, saying of that time, "It was a magnificent epic."

spreading religious beliefs. Few people doubted the stories. Often the myths told of the gods fighting one another and of an entire universe at war with itself.

Another story, the Legend of the Suns, was often told. A creation myth, it was as common to the Aztecs as the story of Adam and Eve is to us. According to the Legend of the Suns, all human beings on earth have already been created and destroyed four times. The first destruction was caused by wild animals, the second by wind, the third by fire, and the fourth by flood. Each of these cycles of death and rebirth were called Suns. The Aztecs believed that they lived in the time of the Fifth Sun. That Sun also was destined to die.

But the dreaded Death of the Fifth Sun could be avoided, or at least delayed, if the gods were pleased with the conduct of men and women. The gods' humor depended on the gifts they received. The highest gift humans could offer to the gods was life itself. Thus the religion established a need for killing people on the altars of the gods. Such human sacrifice was also a way of paying back the gods for past favors. A continuation of the Legend of the Suns said that after the world ended for the fourth time, two gods ventured to the underworld, where people go when they die. They found the bones of men and women and caused them to spring back to life. In the process of rekindling human life, however, the gods died. Those two heroic gods were transformed into the sun and the moon. Human sacrifice was therefore also a means of giving thanks to them.

The All-Powerful Gods

The historian William H. Prescott counted thirteen major gods and goddesses in the Aztec system and at least two hundred lesser ones. Some scholars have numbered up to sixteen hundred gods in the Aztec pantheon. The Aztecs worshiped a god of the winds and a god of fire. Merchants, soldiers, and stonemasons all had their special gods. A god watched over each division of the day—morning, afternoon, and evening. Brewers of *pulque* (PUL-kay), a beer made out of cactus, offered prayers to a god they believed would make their drink tasty and pleasing. Two gods were associated with corn. Centotl (sehn-TOH-tl) was the god of the corn plant, while his sister Xilonen (shih-loh-NEHN) was the goddess of the tender ear. A favorite god among young people was Xochipilli (shoh-chih-PEE-lee), the prince of flowers.

Statues of the gods were found everywhere in the Aztec empire. The figures were made of wood, stone, or clay. The house of a humble worker had almost no furniture at all, but even the poorest family had a crude altar at home. Usually the altar held a statue of Coatlicue (koh-TLEE-kay), the earth goddess. Other statues were placed on rooftops, in front of particularly large trees, at crossroads, at wells or watering holes, and on hilltops. At times the people stood the statues on their heads in order to get the gods' attention. Tlaloc (TLAH-lohk), the rain god, was often placed upside down by farmers praying for rain.

To the farmers Tlaloc was one of the most important gods in the heavens. In Mexico, which is frequently stricken by killer droughts, the rain god's favor was a matter of life and death. According to myths, Tlaloc possessed four jars of water with which he controlled the nation's destiny. One jar contained sweet water and would nurture beautiful crops. Another jar held foul water that caused mold to grow on corn. Still another jar held freezing rain. The last jar contained impure water that clogged the juices of the corn plant and prevented the kernels from maturing. The jar Tlaloc

A huge statue of Tlaloc, the rain god. Since the rains came at his whim, Tlaloc's favor was much sought after by the Aztecs.

Coatlicue, the Earth Mother. Her head is formed by the facing heads of two enormous rattlesnakes.

chose to use depended on how he was treated. And Tlaloc was a cruel deity. While the other gods accepted adults as sacrificial victims, Tlaloc preferred the hearts of children.

On Tlaloc's festival day boys and girls six to eight years old were led to his temple to be killed by his priests. The priests assured the children and their parents that at death the boy or girl would join the god and be happy forever in his house. Still the tears flowed—from the child, his or her family, and from the onlookers. Tears were considered to be a good sign, as they were related to rain. Tlaloc's statue was usually carved with serpentlike fangs at the mouth and eyes that were covered with mysterious goggles. As a god he was respected but never loved.

In addition to their multitude of gods, the Aztecs believed in a divine being who created the universe. This was the same invisible god the poet Nezahualcoyotl embraced in his writings. The divine creator was all powerful, but the people thought of him as being unapproachable. Prayers and sacrifices had to be made to the temple gods. These were personal deities, closer to humans.

The Aztecs held firm beliefs in a life after death. A popular poem said, "When we die it is not true that we die./For still we live./We are resurrected." The priests claimed that thirteen levels of heaven or nine levels of hell awaited a soul at death. The manner of death rather than the conduct of life determined the soul's final judgment. The highest level of heaven was awarded to a man who died in battle or to a woman who died in childbirth. A woman who died trying to give birth was honored by a glorious prayer: "By your labors you have won Our Lord's noble death, glorious death./Truly you have toiled for it, well you merited it." A man or a woman who died on the altars as a sacrificial victim was also welcomed in heaven. The lowliest station in hell was reserved for cowardly soldiers, killed while retreating.

The Priests and the Wizards

Countless priests worked in Aztec society. The historian William Prescott claimed that five thousand priests were assigned to the capital's main temple alone. Most priests were recruited as boys from the *calmecac*, the training schools for the ruling classes. In service they performed a wide range of duties. Priests maintained temple fires and recorded events in the diaries of the empire. At night they studied the heavens, reading the passage of stars so they could properly advise farmers when to plant crops and generals when to wage war. The priests memorized stories from the nation's past and told them to crowds of people. The holy men served as teachers in the school.

A special order of priests performed human sacrifice. Those who regularly executed the sacrificial ritual by cutting out a victim's heart were a fearsome-looking lot. Priestly rules forbade them from cutting their hair or from bathing. Consequently, the blood, squirting from the chests of victims, lodged in their hair in

The pyramids at the ancient and mysterious city of Teotihuacán, about thirty miles northeast of Mexico City. Quetzalcóatl, the plumed serpent, looms in the foreground.

large knots. A Spaniard said of these priests, "They wore black cloaks and hoods. . . . They wore their hair very long, down to their waists, and some even down to their feet, and it was so clotted and matted with blood that it could not be pulled apart."

Aside from the priests there existed a class of men dedicated to fortune-telling, to healing the sick through miracles, and to interpreting dreams. For a fee these wizards would contact a dead relative or look into the future and thus advise a family. The wizards claimed they worked their wonders by entering a supernatural state. To assist them into this divine state they drank *pulque* or they ingested drugs—special mushrooms, peyote cactus, or morning-glory seeds. A Spaniard, observing an Aztec man who had eaten hallucinogenic mushrooms, wrote, "So beside himself and intoxicated was he that . . . he saw visions and revelations of the future, as if the devil spoke to him. . . ."

Magicians and sorcerers also operated in the Aztec world. These were tricksters who, it was said, could change themselves into animals or disappear into thin air when they wished. They lived on the fringe of society and were called upon when a feud caused a neighbor to hate his fellow neighbor. Then the magician was paid to cast spells and put curses on the hated person. The sorcerer thrived in times of desperation but was normally an outcast and feared by the people.

The Cult of Quetzalcóatl

The second tallest pyramid in Tenochtitlán belonged to Quetzalcóatl, the strangest god in the Aztec pantheon. Often he seems more a man than a god. In writing, Quetzalcóatl was described as a feathered serpent. Legends claimed he once lived with the Mexican people. He came to the land from the ocean in the east, sailing on a gigantic ship that looked like a serpent. It was he who taught people how to grow corn. One myth said that before his time the ants had hidden all the world's corn in their nests. Quetzalcóatl turned himself into an ant, entered an anthill, and carried out a kernel to present it to human farmers.

In the days when Quetzalcóatl walked with men and women, a paradise existed on earth. The air was perfumed. Water tasted as sweet as honey. Cotton grew in red, blue, or whatever color the farmer wished. Corn was so huge that one ear was all a man could carry. Naturally the people loved Quetzalcóatl for bringing them this heaven on earth. They wanted to shower him with gifts. But

HOW OLD IS QUETZALCÓATL?

In a pantheon of violent gods, the very humane Quetzalcóatl is unique. It is known he was worshiped by the Toltecs who ruled central Mexico while the Aztecs were still wandering nomads. But probably the cult of Quetzalcóatl predates even the Toltecs. In the 900s the Maya were said to be led by a god-king called Kukulcan, who had many characteristics similar to those of Quetzalcóatl, the Feathered Serpent. Even though his teachings condemning human sacrifice were generally ignored in Mexico, the Feathered Serpent made a profound impact on the country's ancient cultures.

In this Aztec drawing of Quetzalcóatl, the gentle god appears as a man. Like other Aztec deities, Quetzalcóatl had more than one role: He was the feathered serpent; the god of the wind; the god of learning and the priesthood; the master of life.

Quetzalcóatl refused all offerings of human sacrifice. He preferred gifts of beautiful butterflies to bloody human hearts.

The period of bliss ended when Quetzalcóatl developed an enemy. A rival god, Tezcatlipoca (teh-skaht-lih-POH-kah), the "Smoking Mirror," grew jealous of Quetzalcóatl's popularity with humans. The Smoking Mirror was the lord of night, a favorite spirit among sorcerers and evildoers. The two gods fought, a battle that shook the earth. Smoking Mirror won the battle and banished the gentle Quetzalcóatl from Mexico. Quetzalcóatl left the country as he came, riding a serpent-shaped ship over the sea to the east. Prior to sailing, though, Quetzalcóatl vowed to return in the year One Reed and claim the lands of Mexico in his name.

Quetzalcóatl was worshiped by the Toltecs and many other people in ancient Mexico. Before the Aztecs arrived, the Valley of Mexico was dominated by the Toltec people. The Aztecs regarded the Toltecs as the masters of wisdom. They freely borrowed architecture and farming techniques from them. They also borrowed their gods, including the Feathered Serpent.

Even though the Aztecs were rigid in their beliefs, they were also supremely tolerant of opposing religious forces. Quetzalcóatl was the opposite of their most powerful god, the terrible Hummingbird. Quetzalcóatl loathed human sacrifice, while the

Hummingbird demanded it. Yet both gods, with their conflicting needs, were worshiped freely by the people. It was strange that Quetzalcóatl, the gentle god, contributed so directly to the final downfall of the Aztecs when he was confused with the Spanish conquistador, Cortés. The parallels between Quetzalcóatl and Cortés were remarkable. One striking parallel was the fact that Cortés, like the Feathered Serpent, preached against human sacrifice.

Smoking Mirror. The Aztecs made this mask of Quetzalcóatl's rival spirit by embedding pieces of turquoise into a human skull.

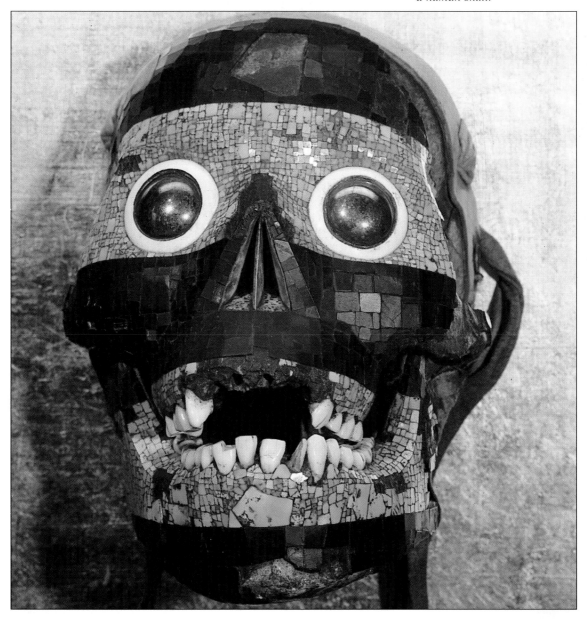

CHAPTER FOUR

WAR, THE DIVINE MISSION OF THE AZTECS

At one time, eight of these life-sized statues lined the steps of the Hummingbird god's temple.

To the Aztecs the sun did not simply rise in the morning. Instead daylight fought the darkness. Over farmers' fields the life-giving forces of rain struggled constantly against the evils of drought. Within every human body, the demons of sickness fought with the angels of good health. The Aztecs found war everywhere—in the cosmos, on earth, and in the underworld. It is only natural that a religion which so embraced war fostered a military society—and it is only natural that the most powerful god in the people's pantheon was the god of war.

Huitzilopochtli, Devourer of Human Hearts

Religion shapes peoples' lives, but people also shape their religion. As the Aztecs struggled to feed their growing population on their rain-starved land, their gods evolved to become commanding figures. One deity, Huitzilopochtli, rose above all others.

When the Aztecs were wanderers, Huitzilopochtli, the Hummingbird spirit, was their god of the hunt. It is easy to picture parties of hunters praying in front of the Hummingbird's idol before going off into the stark desert in search of rabbits or the occasional deer. After the Aztecs settled and began to carve out an empire, the Hummingbird's role expanded—he became the god of war. (Soldiers and hunters often believe they are on similar missions.) Late in Aztec history, the Hummingbird was exalted to even greater heights. Priests made him the sun god, the force of light that clashed with the darkness each morning. The highest pyramid in the Aztec capital was built to honor the Hummingbird. More victims were sacrificed to him than to any other god.

The Spaniards who arrived with Cortés regarded all Aztec gods as devils. They especially hated and feared the Hummingbird, whom they compared to Satan himself. Shortly after they

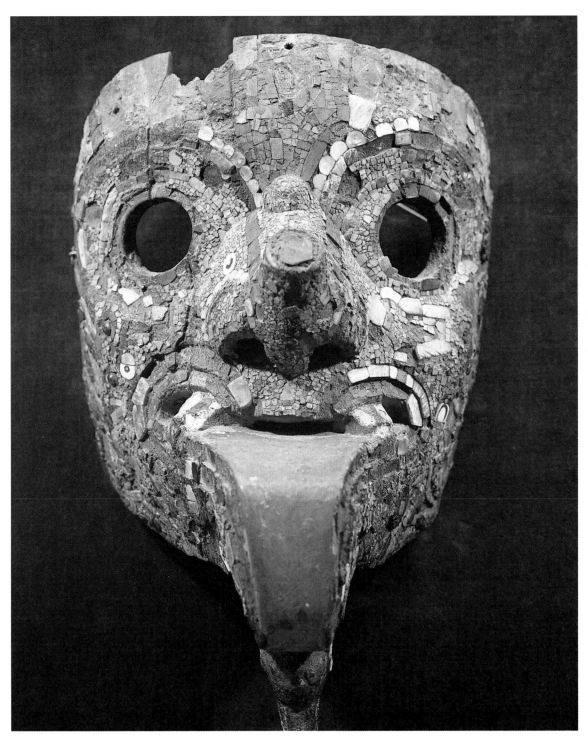

A mask of Xolotla, the evil twin of Quetzalcóatl. The Aztecs used stones, mostly pieces of turquoise, to create the gruesome image.

met, Montezuma gave Cortés and the Spaniards a tour of Tenoch-titlán's temple complex. Upon gazing at the Hummingbird god's statue, Bernal Díaz wrote, "The great idol had round his neck the figures of human heads and hearts. . . ." His temple, according to Díaz, was "besmeared with blood [and] stunk worse than all the slaughter-houses in [Spain]."

In his book Bernal Díaz also preserved a conversation between Cortés and Montezuma concerning Huitzilopochtli and the other gods. Díaz wrote, "Cortés . . . expressed his wonder how so wise a prince [as Montezuma] could worship such absurd and wicked gods. . . . Montezuma showed marks of displeasure at these expressions . . . saying we had insulted their gods who were kind to them, who gave them health and seasonable rains, good harvests, fine weather, [military] victories, and whatever else they desired."

After Cortés seized Montezuma and held him prisoner, the

PYRAMIDS AND TEMPLES

Many societies in the Americas built pyramids—enormous structures with square bases and four triangular sides. One of the greatest of all pyramid complexes was constructed in the Valley of Mexico centuries before the rise of the Aztec people. The Aztecs believed these had been built by the gods, and they named the pyramid city Teotihuacán (tay-oh-tih-wha-KAHN), "Where Men Become Gods." (See page 44.) Unlike those in Egypt, pyramids in ancient Mexico did not cover the burial site of a powerful ruler. It is not certain why the Mexicans of long ago built their pyramids. A recent excavation revealed that the largest pyramid of Teotihuacán was built over an ancient cave that may have been thought of as a holy spot. Aztec pyramids were flat topped and had a temple built on their peaks. A steep staircase led up the pyramid's side to the temple.

Temples served as worship centers for the Aztec people. It was there that the bloody rite of sacrifice was performed. Entrance to some temples was forbidden to all but priests. Generally, temples were small structures of irregular shapes that housed a statue of a god and perhaps a sacrificial stone. Often the temples found on pyramid tops were built of wood. Those made of stone had walls covered with carvings of snakes and gloomy-looking priests. Many temples were on ground level instead of on pyramid tops. Those on the ground were larger structures and usually served several gods, whose statues were carved into the temple wall.

Spaniard ordered the statue of the Hummingbird to be removed from the pyramid top. The idol was replaced with figures of Christian saints. The Aztec people exploded with rage over the desecration of their most powerful god. Shortly thereafter, war broke out between the Aztecs and Spaniards.

The Ultimate Gift to the Gods

Most ancient societies practiced some form of human or animal sacrifice. The Bible tells of Abraham coming to within an inch of sacrificing his son Isaac, only to be stopped at the last moment by a heavenly voice. The Maya people of ancient Central America, whom historians regard as the greatest scholars in the Americas, regularly killed people on their altars to please the gods. But no ancient people took human sacrifice to such ghastly heights as did the Aztecs.

Early in Aztec history human sacrifice was a rare event. Then, sometime in the 1450s, as the empire was expanding, a terrible drought struck the land. The drought lasted four years, destroying the corn crops. Many people thought that the end of the world was at hand. In desperation they turned to their priests. The Aztec holy men claimed the gods needed blood to restore their blessings and bring rain. In a furious few weeks thousands of people were sacrificed. And, through a dreadful coincidence, the rains came, saving the corn. The Aztecs never forgot the power of human sacrifice.

As the Aztec empire grew, so did the numbers of people offered to the gods. When the empire reached its zenith, thousands of human beings each year met their deaths on the altars. In 1490, according to Aztec records, some twenty thousand victims were sacrificed to celebrate the completion of Huitzilopochtli's new pyramid. It was said that during that festival the lines of doomed people stretched two miles outside the city, and the capital stank for weeks thereafter from blood and decaying flesh.

Most sacrificial victims were young men. Often they were taken as "taxes" from cities within the empire. The preferred victims, however, were soldiers captured in war. It was believed soldiers had fierce hearts and would therefore strengthen the gods.

51

The men were well treated until their final, horrible, last moment of life. Many were given drugs to help them make the final walk to the altars without faltering. The victims were told, and most of them believed, that their deaths at the altar would propel them to a wonderful place in heaven.

The sacrificial ritual was a grisly spectacle performed in front of huge throngs of people. Commonly those chosen to die were marched in lines up the pyramid steps to the altar on top. There four priests held the victim face up over a special sacrificial stone. A fifth priest plunged a razor-sharp knife into the victim's chest. The priest then reached into the chest opening and pulled out the heart while it was still beating. Triumphantly the priest held up the bloody heart in front of the statue of the god.

An Aztec drawing of the grim sacrificial ritual. Here prisoners of war are being offered to the Hummingbird god.

These remains of sacrificial victims were unearthed in Mexico City several years ago. The knives used by the priests can still be seen.

All during the gory sacrificial ritual, a priest beat a slow rhythm on a huge snakeskin-covered drum. Bernal Díaz called it an "accursed drum," and said, "nothing can equal the dismal impression its sound conveyed." The ritual drum at Tenochtitlán was taller than a man. Its thunderous beats served to drown out the screams of the victims.

About twenty years after the Spanish Conquest, a Catholic priest asked an elderly man why the old nation practiced human sacrifice on such a large scale. Why, wondered the priest, didn't the people limit their offerings to animals, as did many other societies? The old Aztec man shook his head scornfully. He said only "cheap" people offered animals to their gods. The Aztecs were a great nation. They would not dare to disrespect their gods by giving them the hearts of animals alone.

Leading an Empire

All political power in the Aztec world came ultimately from the emperor. The emperor was not born into his title. Instead, Aztec rulers were elected for life by a body of nobles. The same body of nobles later served as the emperor's advisory council. Descendants of emperors were often elected to the throne. For example, Montezuma's grandfather served as emperor in the mid-1400s. But, unlike European countries, no royal family existed among the Aztecs.

The nobles themselves were called the *pipiltin* (pih-pihl-TEEN), the sons of lords. All *pipiltin* claimed to be related to Acamapichtli (ah-cah-mah-PEESH-tlee), who, in the year 1375, was appointed the first Aztec emperor. Acamapichtli had twenty wives and innumerable sons and daughters. He alone was the father of the Aztec ruling class that dominated society for years to come. The noble *pipiltins* were the nation's principle landowners, and they jealously clung to their powers and their riches. No commoner could be promoted to their ranks. A commoner rose in status only if he proved heroic in battle by capturing many prisoners.

The Aztecs made no distinction between government and religious leadership. To them the laws of the church and those of the state carried the same authority. Montezuma was a high priest as well as being the nation's emperor. He considered himself to be a personal servant of Huitzilopochtli. But never did Montezuma

HUMAN SACRIFICE AND THE SPANIARDS

Spanish soldiers were shocked and disgusted when they witnessed the Aztec priests performing their bloody sacrificial rituals. They said the practice of human sacrifice stood as proof that the Aztecs were a barbaric people. As barbarians, they needed to be defeated in war so they could be "civilized" by the more enlightened Spaniards. But all the men with Cortés had grown up during the Spanish Inquisition, a time of terrible religious excesses in Spain. Probably every soldier had seen men and women condemned as sinners and burned to death at the stake. Death at the stake was, in many ways, a Christian form of human sacrifice. The horrible executions by fire were carried out by priests who claimed they acted in the name of God.

claim kinship with the deity. A ruler was said to be "the mother and father of the empire." It was a position of solemn trust, and a man had to remain humble to the gods to fill the position properly.

The enthronement ceremony of a new emperor illustrates the close relationship between government and religion. First the new emperor punctured his ears, arms, and legs with a sharp needle. This form of self-torture was an almost daily practice among priests. Then the emperor, streaming with blood, entered the throne room of the Hummingbird god. He sprinkled his blood on the altar flame. Humbly he kissed the ground at the idol's feet. When the long and painful ceremony was over, he received his crown—a brightly colored headdress made of the rarest feathers.

All emperors had to have served in the field as army officers. Montezuma himself was a distinguished general. The army, like the priesthood, was a noble body in Aztec eyes.

Warrior of the Gods

Montezuma's father once wrote, "If a war is not going on, the Aztecs consider themselves to be idle." War was the work of the nation. It was also a very real manifestation of the people's religion. A man engaged in battle became a part of the greater war that was taking place perpetually somewhere in the universe. An Aztec writer put his zest for warfare poetically when he said:

> *There is nothing like death in war:*
> *Nothing like the flowery death*
> *So precious to Him who gives life!*
> *Far off I see it! My heart yearns for it!*

A cowardly soldier was punished with death, but rarely did that punishment have to be imposed. Fanatical courage was demanded and received from almost all Aztec boys and young men. The experienced Spanish soldiers, who had fought against Europe's finest armies, were astounded by Aztec bravery. "They [the Aztec soldiers] sprang upon us like lions," wrote Bernal Díaz. Displaying boldness in battle was the only way the common soldier was able to move up in class. Knightly orders of "Jaguars"

A life-sized statue of an Eagle warrior. Eagle warriors were admired as heroes by the Aztecs.

and "Eagles" were honored within the army. Members of those orders were national heroes, men who had taken many prisoners in battle. The Eagles and Jaguars proudly marched at the head of parades, and they enjoyed respect similar to that afforded the ruling class.

The Aztec nation could field a standing army of more than 200,000 regular soldiers. The men were divided into regiments

This Aztec temple, carved out of rock, was dedicated to warriors of the Eagle and the Jaguar ranks.

of eight thousand and subdivided into companies of one hundred. Spears and swords were the primary infantry weapons. The Aztec sword, called a *macuauhuitl* (mah-cuah-HWEE-tl), was a wicked double-edged device whose blade was made of obsidian. Obsidian is a volcanic glass. Soldiers were skilled at honing their obsidian sword blades so sharp they could sever a foe's head in one stroke.

Battles, like religious events, began with a dramatic ceremony. When the Aztec army descended upon a city, the opposing army met it at the city's outskirts. Facing each other, both sides shouted war cries. To the rear, musicians blew on shell trumpets and played flutes made of hollow bones. Both the Aztecs and the enemy armies began their battles with music. In front of the ranks, dancers performed menacing gyrations. Finally a general gave the signal to attack. Soldiers howled and drums pounded as the men rushed their enemy.

Certainly blood was spilled and lives lost in battle, but the object of close-in fighting—when the warriors battled each other hand-to-hand—was to capture a foe so he could later be sacrificed. Killing an opponent was considered to be clumsy and wasteful.

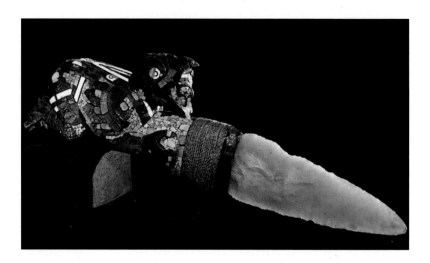

An obsidian knife with an elegant handle, no doubt the work of an Aztec jeweler

Soldiers who took prisoners were awarded special feathers, which they wore in parades. Those who captured many enemy troops became eligible for knighthood.

When an Aztec army overwhelmed a city, its civilian population was rarely harmed. After the surrender, however, the soldiers quickly burned a captive city's main temple and replaced it with one for the worship of the Hummingbird god. The Aztec writing symbol for a conquered city was a pyramid with a spear poked through it. Spreading the influence of the Hummingbird was the divine mission of the Aztec state. After the battle, the doomed city was forced to pay tribute to the Aztec government forever.

Toward the final days of empire, the tribute system and the army fed on each other. From the conquered people the Aztec government demanded tributes of corn, stones for building, obsidian for weapons, and slaves to construct pyramids. This steady supply of tribute freed Aztec men who would normally have to toil as farmers and workers in order to feed the society. Thus freed, the men became soldiers. Consequently the Aztecs were able to support a corps of professional army officers, men who did little more than wage war or prepare for war. The army became so fearfully efficient that many nations or cities simply surrendered the moment Aztec regiments appeared at their borders.

Not all wars were waged for tribute or for territory. Some wars took place for the sole purpose of capturing soldiers to be sacrificed on the altars of Tenochtitlán. These were called "flower wars," because they resulted in giving the gods a beautiful gift. During a flower war the Aztec soldier showed an amazing camaraderie with his enemy. After the battle the wounded were quickly patched up. All prisoners were fed. An Aztec who captured another man in battle was usually privileged to walk him to the sacrificial altar. At the altar he turned the captive over to the priest and said, "Here is my well-beloved son." At that point the captive was supposed to say, "Here is my revered father." A member of the Spanish forces said of these ceremonies, "The victim was no longer an enemy to be killed, but a messenger who was sent to the gods."

This stunning featherwork shield shows a mythical beast holding a sacrificial knife in its jaws. The shield may have been a gift from Montezuma to Cortés.

CHAPTER FIVE

REMINDERS AND REMAINS

No one in central Mexico had ever known an empire mightier than that of the Aztecs. Its territory swept from sea to sea. Its army was invincible. Its gods were the most powerful in the cosmos. So unmovable was the nation that an Aztec poet boasted:

> *Who could conquer Tenochtitlán?*
> *Who could shake the foundation of heaven?*

This powerful sculpture of a jaguar was found long after the Aztecs ceased to rule the Valley of Mexico. In its back is a receptacle, used to hold human hearts during the sacrificial ritual.

But all came to a stunning end before Hernán Cortés and his conquistadores. The Spaniards had firearms that killed at twice the range of an Aztec arrow. They fought with iron swords that shattered the obsidian weapons used by the Aztecs. Also, the Spaniards cleverly enlisted the aid of other Mexican nations who hated the Aztecs because of their constant demand for tributes. The final, terrible battle for Tenochtitlán resulted in the total collapse of the Aztec nation. An Aztec poet surveying the ruins of his capital, lamented:

Broken spears lie in the road;
we have torn our hair in grief.
The houses are roofless now,
and their walls are red with blood.

The Aftermath of the Conquest

Without knowing it the Spaniards brought a deadly ally with them to Mexico. At least one member of Cortés's army had smallpox, a dreaded disease that left Europeans blinded or terribly scarred from sores. The people in the Americas had never been exposed to smallpox. They had not developed a resistance to the disease. While smallpox left Europeans blinded, it killed Native Americans. During the height of battle between Cortés and the Aztecs,

DISEASE AND DIVINE POWER

In the years following the Spanish Conquest no one understood why the Native Americans of Mexico were dying off in such horrible numbers from diseases while the Spaniards seemed so miraculously invulnerable. The Europeans were immune to the sicknesses they brought to the New World, and for this reason stayed relatively healthy. But Spanish priests were quick to claim that their god protected the Spaniards from the evil forces that were striking down Native Americans by the thousands. To the frightened Aztecs, the priests' argument was powerful. Many historians today believe the Native American people readily converted to Christianity in the hope that they too could obtain the protection from sickness that the Spaniards seemed to enjoy.

a smallpox epidemic struck Tenochtitlán. An Aztec wrote, "Sores erupted on [people's] faces, breasts, bellies. They had so many painful sores that they could not move, not even turn over in their beds, and if someone tried to move them they screamed in agony."

Smallpox, measles, and other diseases carried to the Americas by Europeans continued to devastate the Aztec people after the Spanish Conquest. By the 1550s, thirty years after Cortés's invasion, the Native American population in central Mexico had been reduced by half because of rampaging epidemics. Centuries passed before the region was again as thickly populated as it had been under the Aztecs.

The Spaniards incorporated the surviving people into a new empire. They called the empire New Spain, and its capital was Mexico City, once Tenochtitlán. New Spain lasted as a nation for three hundred years before the Mexicans revolted and established the independent state we know today.

The destruction of the Aztec religion was the first order

The remains of an Aztec pyramid and temple near Mexico City. Today it is called the Temple of Santa Cecilia.

of business for the Spaniards after the conquest. Officials of New Spain commanded the Aztec people to totally abandon their old religion and accept Christianity. Spanish priests claimed that the temple gods were devils and worshiping the idols meant that the souls of the Aztecs would burn in hell. It is difficult to imagine how stunned the defeated Aztecs must have felt when listening to the Spaniards. Their new masters demanded they suddenly give up the beliefs that had guided every aspect of their life for generations.

Yet the Aztecs quickly accepted Christian teachings. In the first two years after the conquest, more than one million people volunteered to be baptized by Catholic priests. The priests hailed these conversions as a miracle, but they failed to understand that the Aztecs had always welcomed new gods. The Almighty God preached by the Spaniards was simply given His place in the people's religious order. And, unknown to the Spanish priests, the Aztecs continued to worship their old idols in secret. Farmers hid statues of the rain god in their fields. Workers kept images of the

The Spaniards sometimes built Catholic churches atop Aztec pyramids. This church near the city of Cholula is an example.

earth goddess in dark corners of their houses. No longer were human sacrifices performed for the gods, but people still gave them gifts. In front of the deity's images they left fruit, flowers, or corn cakes.

Most of those who secretly offered gifts to the gods were baptized Catholics. On the surface, New Spain was a Christian society loyal to the Spanish king. But memories of Aztec times still burned in the hearts of the people. Even today, the legacy of the Aztec world lingers over Mexico.

Ghosts of the Aztecs

In modern Mexico City, supermarkets operate that are identical to those in the United States. In mountain towns far from the capital, though, people shop in a different manner. Village markets are ghosts from the past. There, vendors spread goods on the ground on top of pieces of canvas. The Aztecs displayed goods in much the same way. Sellers of vegetables in the village market arrange tomatoes and potatoes in little pyramids. Ancient wall paintings show Aztec vendors forming tiny pyramids with their vegetables.

Modern Mexican markets, such as this one in the city of Oaxaca, are similar to the Aztec markets of old with their beautifully arranged fruits and vegetables.

The village market is the community meeting place, a social center. The Aztecs regarded the market as the heart of their social life.

Also in today's small markets are stalls owned by people who specialize in selling herbs with health-giving powers. The herb seller, *herbero*, offers dried roots or leaves that customers take home, brew into tea, and drink. Signs tell what kind of illness the herb is supposed to cure: FOR SLEEPLESSNESS, FOR NERVOUSNESS, FOR A SOUR STOMACH. These same herbs were sold in Aztec times and reportedly aided people suffering the same sicknesses. One of the herbs available today is called Aztec lily, and the *herbero* says it will reduce fevers.

Folk doctors called *curanderas* still treat people who live in the small towns. The *curanderas,* most of whom are women, roll an egg over a person's body to determine his or her illness. Aztec folk doctors performed a similar ritual. Modern Mexico has pharmacies dispensing the latest medicines and hospitals staffed with well-trained doctors, but many sick people prefer the old ways of restoring their health. The old ways have deep Aztec roots.

In isolated mountain settlements live people who still speak Nahuatl (NAH-huah-tl), the ancient Aztec tongue. For centuries after the arrival of Europeans, the men and the women of far-flung communities clung to the old language, refusing to learn Spanish. Nahuatl is a wonderfully melodic tongue. Many Mexicans, proud of their Aztec heritage, are trying to restore it. However, despite their efforts, the language is dying. Today it is spoken at home mainly by the old people. Children in the villages where it is used call it "Grandma's tongue." Yet some Nahuatl words were long ago incorporated into Spanish and are used practically every day: *tecolote,* "owl"; *cacahuate,* "peanut"; *sintsonte,* "mockingbird"; and a word that is spelled and pronounced pretty

Modern workers cut the cactus plant so it can be made into the alcoholic drink pulque. Aztec society both respected and feared pulque's effects. Drunkards were often sentenced to death.

much the same in Spanish, Nahuatl, and English—*coyote.*

To the south of Mexico City lies the town of Tepoztlán (teh-pahz-TLAHN). It was absorbed into the Aztec empire in the 1400s, but its history dates back further still. Some legends say the gentle god Quetzalcóatl once made his home there. The town sits at the end of a wildly beautiful valley, where mountain streams rush through thick forests. In the forests are the ruins of pyramids and temples once constructed by Aztec workmen. Centuries ago a statue of the god Tepoztecatl (teh-PAHZ-teh-kah-tl) stood in the valley. He was the spirit the brewers prayed to while making *pulque,* the Aztec alcoholic drink. *Pulque,* a cactus beer, is still enjoyed throughout Mexico. The stone figure of Tepoztecatl was

The Aztecs loved their festivals, which usually included special events. One ancient ceremony is still performed in Mexico today—Los Voladores, "The Flyers."

long ago removed, but its base remains. The base plays a major role in an exciting festival celebrated once a year by everyone in the town.

In Aztec times, as well as in the modern era, the people of Tepoztlán held a harvest festival in September. When the Aztecs dominated the region, Tepoztecatl was the local god of the harvest as well as the lord of *pulque.* Today he still does double duty. Townspeople honor him at harvest time, and they drink lots of *pulque* in the process.

The current festival begins with a night parade from the town's center into the mountains where the statue of the god once stood. Marchers in the parade carry torches. As the procession weaves over mountain trails, it looks like a mythical fiery snake. Surely a night parade held in the Aztec period had to look the same. Adding to the mystical effect are musicians. Two old men, one playing a flute and the other beating on a drum, follow the marchers. The ancient mood of the festival changes when the people set off rockets and light firecrackers. The drama shifts back to the town square, where a loud band begins to play. We know now we have returned to modern times, because practically every number blasted from the band is an American rock-and-roll piece.

Shadows of Tenochtitlán

Many population experts believe that modern Mexico City is the largest city in the world. Tenochtitlán was, most likely, the largest city in the world five hundred years ago. Mexico City was built over the ruins of old Tenochtitlán. Hernán Cortés ordered his designers to lay out the new city along the lines of the old. Cortés built his own elegant home on the same grounds where Montezuma's palace once stood. In the center of today's city the Metropolitan Cathedral rises near the site of the Hummingbird god's pyramid.

In the heart of Mexico City is a broad plaza called the Zócalo (SOH-cah-loh). It is here the people gather to celebrate events of great importance, such as Mexican Independence Day on September 16. The grounds also served as a rallying place for Aztec celebrations. The Aztecs believed the area that is now the

This Aztec temple was excavated from the grounds of the Zócalo, the plaza in the heart of Mexico City.

Zócalo was a sacred spot. It was there their ancestors first saw the eagle perched on a cactus while eating a snake.

The neighborhood surrounding the Zócalo is steeped in history. Montezuma first met Cortés at a spot just off the square. Cortés is buried in the basement of a centuries-old building in the Zócalo region called the *Hospital de Jesus.* The Spanish flag flew above the Zócalo for three hundred years before the people proclaimed independence in 1821. Today a band plays the Mexican national anthem every morning, and soldiers hoist the Mexican flag. In the center of that flag is the symbol of Mexico: an eagle sitting on a cactus, eating a snake.

Under the busy streets of the Zócalo neighborhood lie the remains of the pyramids, temples, and houses that once served the Aztecs. During the centuries that followed the conquest, workers digging for construction projects have made some startling discoveries. As early as 1790 ditchdiggers chanced upon an immense circular stone covered with beautifully carved figures and Aztec.

glyphs. A glyph is a picture symbol that represents an idea. With great effort the workers hauled the stone to the surface and found that it was twelve feet in diameter and weighed twenty-five tons. It was the great Aztec Calendar Stone, and its inscriptions record the nation's history. The Calendar Stone once stood in the temple of Huitzilopochtli until the Spaniards unceremoniously dumped it on the ground when they dismantled the pyramid.

Construction of the Mexico City subway (the Metro) in the late 1960s and early 1970s yielded a great harvest of Aztec relics. A team of archaeologists watched over the crews digging the subway. Under a street near the Zócalo, workers found a small temple that, when carefully dug out, looked unchanged from the days of Montezuma. Rather than move the rare find, subway engineers designed a station around it. Now when passengers wait for trains at the Piño Suarez stop on the Mexico City Metro, they gaze through windows at a remarkably preserved 500-year-old place of worship.

A prize never found was the Aztec national treasure. Much of that treasure was stolen by the Spaniards who first arrived in Tenochtitlán. However, Cortés and his men believed that the leaders of the empire had hidden a vast store of gold and precious

The famous Aztec Calendar Stone was found under the streets of Mexico City by crews digging a basement in 1790. Many scholars object to the name Calendar Stone to describe this twenty-five-ton disc. Because the image of the sun god is at its center, scholars think it should more properly be called the Sun Stone. Picture writing (glyphs) on the great stone traces Aztec history and tells of prophecies of the gods.

stones somewhere in the old city. The Spanish chief had the last emperor, Cuauhtémoc, tortured to force him to turn over the fortune. Spanish soldiers held Cuauhtémoc's feet in a fire while Cortés demanded that he reveal the hiding place. Cuauhtémoc refused to disclose the information. The emperor took the secret of the treasure with him to his grave. Perhaps no such treasure ever existed, but the Mexican people believe the story and still honor Cuauhtémoc's brave resistance to torture. Most Mexicans are convinced the treasure remains buried somewhere beneath the streets of downtown Mexico City.

The most complete collection of Aztec works is found in the National Museum of Anthropology. The huge Calendar Stone is one of the museum's prize exhibits. Opened in 1964 the museum stands in Mexico City's Chapultepec Park. Today the park is a thousand-acre refuge of grass and trees in the midst of the capital's

Engineers constructing the Mexico City subway in the 1970s discovered this beautifully preserved temple in the Zócalo neighborhood. They decided to build a subway station around it.

The National Museum of Anthropology, one of the world's greatest history museums, opened in Mexico City in 1964. Just before the museum was completed, an enormous sixty-ton statue of Tlaloc, the rain god, was taken from an old Aztec town called Coatlinchan (kwat-leen-CHAN) and transported to Mexico City to be displayed permanently at the museum's entrance. The statue had rested undisturbed in Coatlinchan for more than five hundred years. The villagers warned of dire consequences when government officials had the huge idol moved. Just days after workers put the statue on the museum grounds, a terrible rainstorm struck Mexico City. It was the worst nonrainy-season downpour that anyone could remember.

crowded buildings. Hundreds of years ago the land was infested by snakes. It was there a king once gave the wandering Aztecs permission to build a camp. The king hoped the snakes would kill off the offensive tribe. Instead the Aztecs thrived by eating the snakes. Chapultepec is now the capital's playground. Its most popular attraction, the Anthropology Museum, draws 1.5 million visitors a year.

A less famous museum is the Museum of Mexico City in the Zócalo neighborhood. Exhibits in the museum trace the history of Mexico City from the Aztec period and contain striking paintings and models showing how old Tenochtitlán looked. The museum building is a house whose walls were constructed in Cortés's time. Its cornerstone is taken from an Aztec temple and bears a carved figure of the god Quetzalcóatl. Some history experts believe that Cortés himself supervised the placing of the cornerstone on the foundation back in the 1520s. It is the city's most dramatic example of a building still standing that was constructed from stones taken out of the Aztec walls.

In modern times the greatest discovery came when subway workers near the Zócalo found the remains of a pyramid. Further digging revealed it was the largest Aztec structure yet uncovered from old Tenochtitlán. Archaeologists named it Templo Mayor (TEHM-ploh mah-HOHR), "Main Temple." Serious work to excavate the ruins at the Templo Mayor site began in 1978. When the task was near completion, a fence was erected around the area, and it was transformed into an outdoor museum. Every day visitors enter this living museum, climbing steps and crossing walkways built in an era that now seems magical.

Traffic roars over the streets surrounding the ruined pyramid at Templo Mayor. In the background, glass-and-steel buildings pierce the sky. Here Mexico City meets Tenochtitlán. The thousands of visitors streaming in and out of Templo Mayor serve as a reminder that Mexicans will never forget their ancient history. The Aztecs built a society that overwhelms and often shocks people of the present age. The influence of that society has shaped modern Mexico. Since the Spanish Conquest, the nation has lived with one foot in the western world and another in its golden past. As the Mexican philosopher Octavio Paz said, "Any contact with the Mexican people, however brief, reveals that the ancient beliefs and customs are still in existence beneath western forms."

The remains of the sacrificial altar of Templo Mayor ("Main Temple") make an eerie contrast with the buildings of modern Mexico City.

The Aztecs: A Chronology

300–900   A mysterious people construct a huge pyramid complex about thirty miles from present-day Mexico City at Teotihuacán.

900–1200   The Toltec Empire controls the Valley of Mexico.

1248   The Aztecs enter the Valley of Mexico after a long period of wandering in the deserts of the north.

1325   The Aztecs build the city Tenochtitlán on an island in Lake Texcoco.

1450   Tenochtitlán has seventy thousand inhabitants, making it one of the world's largest cities at the time. Its population continues to grow.

1500   The Aztec empire ranges over central Mexico from the Gulf of Mexico to the Pacific Ocean.

1502   Montezuma II becomes the Aztec emperor.

1510–1518   The Aztecs believe certain occurrences, such as a mysterious comet that hung for many nights in the sky, foretell the return of Quetzalcóatl to claim Mexico as his own.

1518   Tenochtitlán's population has grown to more than 150,000 inhabitants.

1519   Hernán Cortés arrives, and the Aztecs believe he is the god Quetzalcóatl. Cortés seizes Montezuma and holds him captive.

1520   The Aztecs revolt and drive the Spaniards out. Cuauhtémoc becomes the last Aztec emperor.

1521   Cortés regroups and Tenochtitlán is destroyed and the Aztec empire defeated.

1522   The Spaniards begin to build Mexico City over the rubble of Tenochtitlán.

GLOSSARY

camaraderie (come-uh-RAHD-uh-ree): goodwill and agreement among friends

causeway: a raised roadway. In the case of the Aztecs the causeways connected the island city of Tenochtitlán to the main land

city-state: a combination of two terms, city and state. A city-state is a small territory that includes one independently governed city and its nearby surroundings

cosmos: the universe, taken as a whole

cult: a group of people greatly devoted to a particular god or religious belief

curandera: a folk doctor who uses ancient methods to ease the sufferings of sick people

deity: a god or a goddess

desecration: the act of scorning or abusing a sacred object or a belief

emissaries: agents sent out by one party to negotiate with another party

glyph: a picture or symbol that stands for an idea; the Aztecs used glyphs instead of letters in their written language

herb: a plant valued as a medicine or used to enhance the taste of food

idol: an image, often a statue, of a god

interpreter: one who translates orally from one language to another

knightly: pertaining to the word *knight.* A class of soldiers revered for their heroism and their manners

pictographic: describing a written language that uses pictures to convey meanings

pious: describes a person who is extremely devoted to his or her religion

puritanical: having a sternly moralistic attitude toward life

sacrifice: an offering to the gods

seasonal: describes an occurrence that happens during a particular season in a year

tribute: a gift or payment demanded by a conquering nation

vassals: subjected people or states, which are dominated by a more powerful lord or nation

zenith: the highest point of a path or a course

FOR FURTHER READING

Beck, Barbara. *The Aztecs*. New York: Franklin Watts, 1983.

Berdan, Frances. *The Aztecs*. New York: Chelsea House, 1988.

Bierhorst, John, ed. *The Hungry Woman: Myths and Legends of the Aztecs*. New York: Morrow, 1993 (new edition).

Brown, Dale, ed. *Aztecs: Reign of Blood and Splendor*. Alexandria: Time-Life, Inc., 1992.

Burell, Roy. *Montezuma and the Aztecs*. Milwaukee: Raintree, 1992.

Dineen, Jacqueline. *The Aztecs*. New York: New Discovery, 1992.

Gaudiano, Andrea. *Azteca: Story of a Jaguar Warrior*. Boulder: Roberts Rinehart, 1992.

Marrin, Albert. *Aztecs and Spaniards*. New York: Atheneum, 1986.

Mathews, Sally S. *The Sad Night: The Story of Aztec Victory and Spanish Loss* (a work of fiction). New York: Clarion Books, 1993.

Stein, R. Conrad. *The Enchantment of the World: Mexico*. Chicago: Childrens Press, 1984.

Stein, R. Conrad. *The World's Great Explorers: Hernando Cortés*. Chicago: Childrens Press, 1991.

Townsend, Richard. *The Aztecs*. New York: Thames & Hudson, 1992.

BIBLIOGRAPHY

Brundage, Burr Cartwright. *A Rain of Darts*: *The Mexican Aztecs.* Austin and London: University of Texas Press, 1972.

Coe, Michael. *Mexico.* New York: Frederick Praeger Press, 1962.

Covarrubias, Miguel. *Indian Art of Mexico and Central America.* New York: Alfred A. Knopf, 1957.

Davies, Nigel. *The Aztec Empire.* Norman: University of Oklahoma Press, 1987.

Díaz, Bernal del Castillo. *The True History of the Conquest of Mexico.* New York: Farrar, Straus, 1956.

Fehrenbach, T. R. *Fire and Blood: A History of Mexico.* New York: Macmillan, 1973.

Innes, Hammond. *The Conquistadores.* New York: Alfred A. Knopf, 1969.

Kandell, Jonathan. *La Capital: The Biography of Mexico City.* New York: Random House, 1988.

Paz, Octavio. *The Labyrinth of Solitude.* New York: Grove Weidenfield Press, 1985.

Prescott, William. *History of the Conquest of Mexico.* New York: Random House, 1966.

White, Jon Manchip. *Cortés and the Downfall of the Aztec Empire.* New York: Carroll and Graf, Inc., 1971.

Zorita, Alonso de. *Life and Labor in Ancient Mexico.* New Brunswick, New Jersey: Rutgers University Press, 1971.

INDEX

Page numbers for illustrations are in boldface

ABOUT THE AUTHOR

R. Conrad Stein was born and grew up in Chicago. After serving in the Marine Corps he attended the University of Illinois, where he received a degree in history. He later earned an advanced degree from the University of Guanajuato in Mexico. The author lived in Mexico through most of the 1970s, and now the Stein family spends each summer in the town of San Miguel de Allende, which is north of Mexico City. Mexican history has long fascinated Mr. Stein, and he is particularly interested in the Aztec era. Mr. Stein has published more than eighty books for young readers. He lives in Chicago with his wife and their daughter, Janna.